Best of Both Worlds

THE JOURNEY OF MY BODY AND SOUL
SPOKEN THROUGH WORDS

Poetry by 'INTRIGUE'

Doan, Dustin, 1977-
Best of Both Worlds–The Journey of My Body and Soul Spoken Through Words.
ISBN-10: 0-98336-161-4
ISBN-13: 978-09833-61-619

First Edition: October 2011
1

Printed in the United States of America.

Greenbelt
Publishing

This book is dedicated to my daughter, Kebi Marie Doan.
My goal as a parent is to give you unconditional love
as well as unabbreviated discussions of life. You are the definition
of purpose. I love you as deep as the ocean canyons below,
and as true as the earth's atmosphere glows.

FORWARD

Words are a powerful form of both written and verbal expression. In a world where men are often unwilling to explore the deepest and darkest aspects of past and present transgressions, this book proves those stereotypes wrong. In this literary masterpiece, the world gets a rare glimpse into the mind and soul of the poet Intrigue. Readers get to know a man who has risen above adversity and been humbled by life's most eye-opening circumstances. The book offers a clear and uncut analysis of the multiple aspects of family life, scars of past loves, spirituality and the pursuit of happiness. You will find yourself in the middle of an emotional journey that often feels as revealing as staring at your own reflection in the mirror. This book leaves an everlasting impression on what it is like to embrace humility after pretending it is possible to avoid befriending it.

~A.M. MORGAN
3 Morgan Publishing

CONTENTS

INTRO

Thank you for picking up a copy of "Best Of Both Worlds: The Journey Of My Body And Soul, Spoken Through Words." My life has been a rollercoaster. Trouble seeks me out, catching me even during my greatest escape attempts. Maybe trouble feels at home with me. Love? Well, there are stories to tell there as well.

Nevertheless, I continue to grow. When knocked down, I stand back up and dust myself off. I place one foot in front of the other and increase my stride. Refusing to stop will conquer anyone or anything.

Life has also brought success through humility. Mistakes are the greatest teacher. The lessons have not been taught without pain. I have hurt others. In life's process, the greatest damage was done to me. The way I reconcile my actions and capture relief from my torment is by not letting those mistakes go in vain.

My life is and has always been an open book. The following poems capture some of these journeys, both high and low. My greatest desire is to connect with you through this medium.

"LIVE LIFE" is my motto because life demands adventure. Please join me through this journey of my heart and soul. Each of the following poems possesses a distinct part of my being.

Art In Its Written Form

Art has surrounded us for thousands of years. Since early civilizations, written art forms have been practiced. The ancient Egyptian's hieroglyphic writings began a tradition of expressing the physical world through literary tales. Early Europeans wrote magnificent plays to be acted out on stage. The Bible includes a collection of poems among its miraculous stories and deep lessons. From history books to trendy magazines, writing is a necessary expression of life. Writing is a human experience.

Poetry is a creative expression of emotions. As a method to project feelings and interpret experiences, poetry is an exceptional art form. Poetry has become my greatest asset in sharing the celebration of life while offering a clear path to safely share my greatest pain. My struggles release. My obstacles flatten. My triumphs are shared with victory. Poetry has an uncanny way of giving me permission to remember my past as well as dream of my future. In other words, these poems are not made-up stories of the person I thought I was. These poems are a reconciliation of a man and his past. A father and his daughter's future. A lover and his best and worst intentions.

Experience shapes who we are as people. No moment fails to make an impression. Whether it is a beautiful dream or nightmares keeping us up at night, we process our experiences.

Every single person possesses the ability to express their journey through poetry. Poetry is a magnificent art form because it is accessible. A poem can be written for any purpose. Whether for personal growth or sharing with friends and family, poetry offers an opening to real discussions about life. At its greatest, poetry is fundamentally the art of expression. If we are careful, we can inspire. My goal is to trigger deep emotions within my soul, and in turn my audience. The deeper we allow ourselves to go with this medium, the greater our chances become to embrace all of the differences between us.

Words move mountains. The power of words equally enables us to find our individuality and yet find a way to compromise. In order to move society forward, we must struggle to achieve greater understanding to help create a better place for our children.

Poetry brings life into these words. Poetry has a history of tradition and form. The following poems do not adhere to these rules. The highest level of order is to capture emotion. My current work doesn't confine itself to a specific pattern. At different moments in the following poems, my perception and position change. Some of the following poems span more than a decade in life experience.

~INTRIGUE

THE POEMS

HUMILITY

I admire people
Who embrace humility
And have a vision
Of their own mortality
Once you have encountered
Defeat and pain
It is your time to
Expand and gain
Wisdom which increases
Your inner flame
Burning you can
now develop
Into the main
Objective
Which by far
Is to love yourself
For who you truly are
Now I've broken down
Laws and walls
And I accept myself
Flaws and all
No matter what mistakes I've made
Or careless games I've played
I can lay claim
To the fact that I have truly
Experienced shame
Unpretentious behavior
Is my personality

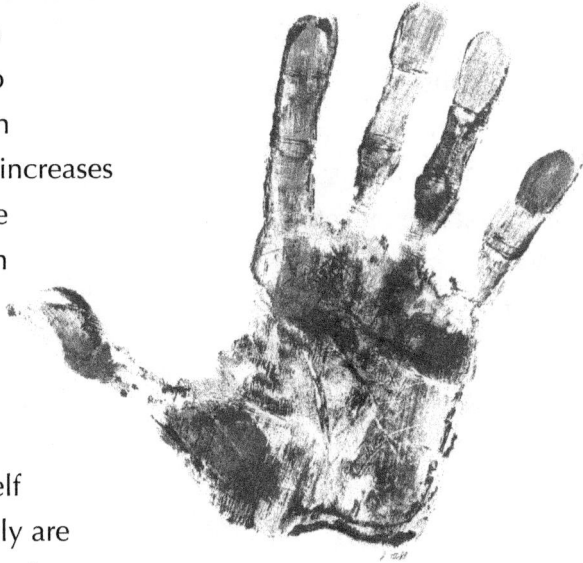

For the rest of this life
That doesn't mean I'll act passive
By any means
Or always do right
But I want to get up
Get out and do something
And I won't let this world
Pass me by
I strive
To stay alive
And I shine bright
Like stars in a cluster
Nothing like the fearful
Who live a quiet life
That lacks luster
So the weak can huddle
Together
Complain and struggle
Fill each other's heads
With negative thoughts
Scrutiny
And they can set forth
A carefully plotted
Mutiny
But I'll stand alone
Comfortably see
Cause I am just a man
If I'm cut I will bleed
I am now modest
I throw my hands up and concede
Pride and arrogance

Capture the hearts of men
And I will no doubt screw up
And sin again
But I accept this without frustration
I used to believe I'd be taken violently
By spontaneous combustion
Burst into flames
While I'm alone at home
Discovered days later
As a pile of ashes
On my mattress
But I had a dream
Of what is to come
Maybe it's a vision
A premonition
I can't see the future necessarily
But I have an intuition
And the rest of my life
Exceeds all expectation
I don't need anyone's opinion
To determine who I am
You see I have accepted humility
Cause I am just a man

CRUSH

Let's see,
Love at first sight?
No, More like,
I'm in flight...

An eagle soaring high,
Upon the thermal air,
Effortlessly,
Without a care...

You are true beauty,
Inside and out,
I will scale the tallest structure,
And shout it out...

I dream of you,
Day after day,
The truth about you,
Is so easy to convey...

I wonder if you would,
Love to hear it,
How you stimulate my mind,
Body and spirit...
Your voice sounds
Like a symphony,
An orchestra playing,
In perfect harmony...
The chemicals released,
In my body from this crush,
Are addicting and intoxicating,
I'm high and it's a rush...

As you strut,
With your head held high you arouse,
Things inside of me that according to physics,
Are not even allowed...

Though these sensations,
Remind me of young adolescence,
You're a fully mature woman,
That has a recognizable presence...

When I think of you,
The grass becomes greener, the sky more blue,
I have had countless fantasies,
Of romancing you...

To never actually have you,
Is a thought so cruel,
You are my mission,
Even if I have to break every rule, but it's cool...

I will be patient,
And lay low in the trenches,
While you go to war with guys that can't actually,
Get you the drink that quenches...

Your thirst,
You know that deep down desire,
A flame burns inside of me for you,
I feel an actual fire...

My heart races,
I forget to breath,
With the thoughts of what you and I,
Could possibly achieve...

Reality,
I don't know you that well,
But on a scale of one to ten,
You are a twelve...

Truth,
You are gorgeous no doubt,
But it's the words you speak and the depth in your eyes,
That my crush revolves around...

I want you, oh my god,
I want you crush,
If we were playing poker,
Then you're the royal flush...

Actually you're an even better hand,
Than that never mind,
There's only one-way to describe you,
You're a one of a kind...

I dream of you,
And every moment I do,
Is similar to the first day of spring,
All the flowers are in bloom...

I want to protect you,
I clinch my fist,
If anyone hurts you,
Their health is at risk...

You see I am here,
Waiting in the wings,
For our moment together,
For whatever it brings...

MY PARENTS

MY PARENTS

I know I'm young mom,
But I really love this man too,
Courtney and I want y'all to get married,
Not later but soon...

I've already forgotten,
About what's his name,
Maybe he's not to blame,
But he damn well better feel shame...

So we are again,
A family of four,
I know mom was panicking,
But now she seems secure...

You want to adopt us?
Dad,
You are my dad now,
You are my sister's dad now...

The judge allowed it,
And it's forever set in stone,
I feel so blessed,
I have received your last name of Doan...

It seems there is peace love and happiness,
Here at 9346 Hathaway,
But just like all good things,
This too must come to an end one day,
You two will argue, fuss and fight,
This dream right into a nightmare,

It's 3am and my little sister is standing,
Next to my bed trembling with fear...

Dust, Dust,
Something's happening listen,
We creep to the door and slowly push it open,
Both fearing what we are about to witness in the kitchen...

It's mom and dad,
Gripping each other's throats,
They're both naked,
Sweating and soaked...

WHAT THE HELL?
STOP IT!
STOP IT!
WHAT THE HELL ARE Y'ALL DOING?

Ok maybe it's the alcohol,
Or maybe he's pulled this anger out of my mom,
She wasn't like this before, maybe,
This is how she's survived the tumultuous relationship this
long...

While I talk to my parents,
My teeth are chattering,
We love you both, but why do we have to continually hear,
yelling,
Stuff getting broken, doors slamming and glass shattering?

Oh really?
Divorce?
Well who are we going to live with?
Oh, Mom of course.

It doesn't stop,
Even though their now separated,
The drama continues,
I'm torn easily, perforated...

Neither will bend,
Or admit they're at fault,
Dad should be locked up,
For physical and verbal assault...

Mom!
Why do you talk like that about dad?
Dad!
Why do you talk like that about mom?

I'm tired of 20 questions!
I'm tired of the interrogations,
Do I look like I care about either one,
Of your feelings or reputations?

Do you two recognize what you are doing to us two?
We are children, wait I take that back,
We are young adults now at eleven and twelve,
Because of everything you two just exposed us to...

I am so angry that my level of respect has diminished
Into every sarcastic comment that pops out of my mouth,
And through my rebellion,
Will be the way I pay back this overdrawn account...

The long-term effects result,
In the fact that I am now colder,
Don't ever ask me why I am, how I am,
And don't ever ask me how I got this chip on my shoulder...

MY PARENTS

You see, I wasn't conceived by my parents,
Through sex, love or planning,
It was later that I was born in a house,
Full of anger, violence and misunderstanding…

Now that I'm older,
And a parent myself,
It's clear my parents,
Were only into themselves…

Breaking this cycle of violence in the home is my goal,
My daughter will have beautiful memories of her childhood,
Because memory,
Is the personal journalism of the soul...

REASONS

He saved me,
After my life had fallen to pieces,
I have reasons,
To believe in Jesus…

Traveling on this journey,
Through dark and light,
Everyone vanished yet Jesus,
Remained to help me fight…

There are highs and lows,
Our bond forever grows,
He has walked next to me my entire life,
Only Jesus knows...

He is the one true salvation,
A star shining bright,
Undeniably the single path,
To everlasting life…

He saved me,
After my life had fallen to pieces,
I have reasons,
To believe in Jesus…

Before I was born again,
Problems consumed my mind,
Every day He performs miracles,
Magnificent and kind…

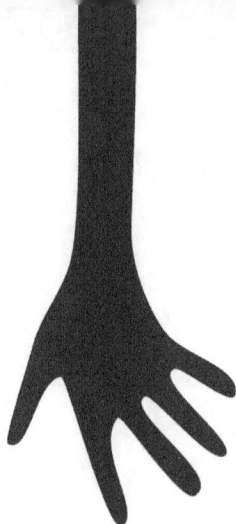

Saved by His almighty hand,
No longer blind,
I feel His spirit around me,
Jesus is divine…

Now I'm equipped,
With a shield and a knife,
Battling against all evil,
Preparing for eternal life…

He saved me,
After my life had fallen to pieces,
I have reasons,
To believe in Jesus…

This is my new life,
Confidently I wear it,
The Holy Trinity,
Father, Son and Holy Spirit...

I must believe,
So into faith I leap,
He is my shepherd,
I am His sheep…

Strength and serenity,
His Church helps us cope,
Infinity and divinity,
Jesus is our hope...

He saved me,
After my life had fallen to pieces,
I have reasons,
To believe in Jesus…

MISREPRESENTATION

MISREPRESENTATION

My god this is fraud…

The way you described yourself in the beginning when we started dating,
Was a church going, private schooling, appreciates family type girl that didn't immediately give up the loving…

It only took those qualities to have me baited like a hook as I shook the other beauties that most definitely deserved a look…

You had what I wanted with the looks sense of humor and personality absolutely recruiting my interest licking my lips and drooling…

In return you made it clear that I appeared to have everything required to hire me as your full time friend and lover even buying me expensive new attire…

In no time flat you were all up on my lap telling me with an eye to eye stare these vibes are unique and rare, you proclaim your loving everything about me right now, which sold me and made me proud, I was up on a cloud, higher than nine in fact I was in a whole new realm cause you're the answer to my prayers after baby mama's hell…

However you're still doing your best impersonation of a player as you spent the night with him, lying about where you've been, which certainly was going to send, me out the door for sure and on to dating again, but you had to pretend, that you were ready to go steady…

You say let's just let bygones be bygones and allow this to all fly by and I frustratingly (hard sigh) sigh...

Negative happenstance as you prance around as if your past is your past knowing damn well that it's not forgot, you've got my heart clogged and it's nasty now I'm in need of an angioplasty, and I obviously haven't put it behind me nor will I, but you have so many amazing qualities that I can't get you off my mind...

So this hope I will nurse while I look the other way and dive into this relationship foolishly head first with the thirst of your potential...

We somehow do seem to grow closer and my god mama I love you so deeply and it's real and I can feel our true love growing still...

The way you constantly glare through me and directly into my soul you know what's in here and as you glow and we grow a little more each day I pray that I can forgive you for the lie, in my face about another guy...

You know what? Now you have forced me to do what I hate and start to insinuate and incriminate and peruse the mystery of your history of faithfulness in your previous relationships...

So here I go, so, have you ever cheated before? Whoa! Every boyfriend you've ever had except your first one? Oh...

Damn I was duped just scoop my jaw up off the ground it's revealed you've been around and around....

I'm out of here no looking back cause you clearly lack, the

most necessary attributes I shoot the deuce, no need to call truce you don't deserve a proper close I want to be far far away from you, but I froze...

Because of your relentless effort to prove to me that you would never again put hurt on me so here I go, I will give you the benefit of the doubt because let's face it you know about the fact that you're the first girl I've ever been faithful to and it's no doubt I will continue to do so through and through...

Ok we will make this work we are only people, I allow myself to trust you again and even frequent your family's church under the steeple...

However it's relevant that something scandalous and malevolent is revealed, it's a fact on how you allow guys from work to talk to you and mack, it's damn near a welcomed attack...

Now I know just as well as anybody that getting hit on and flirting is exciting and inviting however you begged me to stay but the deceit remains and replays over and over and pounds against my thoughts like waves...

I tell you damn near every other day that you're clearly not at the maturity level nor the morality level to claim monogamy and honestly believe me I can see straight through your little smoke screen...

By that I mean your underdeveloped allow me to embellish by saying "This is your sin!" and if I had a pen I would go back and rewrite everything that just occurred or better yet I'd use a pencil with an eraser but you'd still be as transparent as fresh water melted from a glacier...

You are a deceiver and now I'm even a stronger believer in the fact that you disgust me and trust me...

I moved on simply stated forcefully reiterated right here for you to be obliterated incinerated and hated never again will this be debated because I concentrated on the hatred which has finally now deflated thank god we never officially mated I dodged that trap you misrepresented and baited which had my mind dislocated and isolated from the very cautiously created like I said fortunately it's faded and now stated that the punishment made it directly to me, but I go out rated number one because this is your bad karma, mine has become eliminated...

THIS IS JUST SEX...

You hit me with a text,
So I respond back,
You state you love my blue eyes,
And want to touch my six-pack...

The conversation
becomes,
Progressively
bold,
And I let
you know,
I want to
hold...

Your
naked
body,
Next
to my
naked
body,
Ever since I
met you,
It's what
I've been plotting...

Let me come over,
On the late night hour,
Understand that this is just sex,
Rinse off in the shower...

So much sexual tension,
Before the main event,
Tonight's going to get so buck wild,
We'll need to repent...

I'm on my way over,
Let the anticipation build,
I tell you to answer the door wearing,
Only your sexiest pair of heels...

As we stand in the foyer,
Only lit by moonlight,
We kiss passionately,
This is only one night...

We don't make it halfway down the hall,
Before we lose control,
It's just like a fire baby,
We stop drop and roll....

Your skin is so soft,
And I kiss every inch,
Slowly but surely,
I work my way back to your lips....

You're aggressive,
Just as I expected,
And the heat and wetness,
Are instantaneously ingested...

Uuuggghhh,
I love how you taste,
As your creativity is revealed,
All inhibitions are erased...

The evidence,
Starts to flow,
That your losing control,
And about to explode…

Yes! Yes! Yes!
Echoes of the walls,
Then I flip you over,
Now you're on all four paws…

We are like two lions now,
Growling and roaring loud,
I began working it slowly,
But now I'm starting to pound…

I know you're clearly finished,
But I'm not quite done,
I came to smash so the memory will last,
And now your bell is rung…

I pick you up,
Put you over my shoulder,
Walk you down the hall into the bathroom,
And I turn on the shower…

The steam and hot water,
Increase the virtuous ambiguity,
And giving you pleasure,
Is my honor now and responsibility…

We dry off,
Slide under the covers,
I thought this was going be one night,
But clearly we are lovers…

You see the connection two people,
Can create with great sex,
Can intertwine two souls,
At an amazing level that's complex...

Now I'm sitting here asking myself,
What's coming next,
I stand corrected,
Because this is more than just sex...

EVIL LURKS

Evil lurks,
Shadows try to grab and scratch,
But I'm equipped with utilitarian weapons,
The devil is no match…

I'm skillful,
As I traverse with strategic tactics,
Evil is always lurking,
So I've had plenty of time to practice...

He's a relentlessly arriving,
Tsunami in the dark,
However there's a strategically placed lighthouse,
Protruding from the rocks...

This bright light,
Cuts through the storm revealing land,
My foundation of piers and solid beams,
Suspend me over quicksand...

My body is my temple,
And it's architecturally designed,
To withstand hurricane force winds,
In a category five...

I pay close attention,
And try to minimize mistakes,
While the earth shakes,
From the frequent and powerful quakes...

My soul is comfortably in my body,
Stocked and ready for any disaster,
Shadows conjure up evil plots,
Masked as man made and natural...

These moments pop up,
Seemingly unexpectedly,
But I have faith in God, His Son,
And his Son's family...

I carry knowledge of,
Power, equality and love,
God shines His light down on me,
From heaven above...

I am never fearful, always confident,
And a bit unpredictable,
My faith has me ready for his nasty tricks,
The devil is so capable...

I am here forever,
My soul thrives in this life and the next,
Because let's face it,
Eternity is what we're actually up against....

I've seen evil lurking,
While I'm awake and sleeping,
You can count on that indefinitely,
The grim one is always reaping...

PROGRESSION

A blissful evening as I recline,
And listen to the wind blow,
Captured by the chime hanging,
Near my patio...

Signaling the changing,
Of a season,
I reflect on the significant moments,
More reasons...

To thank God,
For every new day,
My life has changed,
In a number of ways...

Calculated moves,
That I set forth months before,
Now it feels,
Like a lifetime ago or more...

My deep inhale (breathe in/breathe out),
And slow exhale mark my new beginning,
I visualize my future,
So grateful to be living...

Goals have been reached,
Now there is more available space,
For the new goals,
To replace the old ones, erased...

A strong grasp,
On where I came from,
Aware of where I am now,
And who I aspire to become...

My life now is a culmination,
Of the carefully plotted steps before,
I will not ignore,
That deep in my core...

I am a similar me,
But this new me,
Is improved because,
I am progressing steadily...

As I now embark across,
An ocean of the unknown,
This trip will be like those before,
But much better equipped as I roam...

Through valleys and mountains,
Over speed bumps and potholes,
Rivers calm and raging,
One ways and forks in the road...

I will crush these obstacles,
I'm strapped up and booted,
They're no match for wisdom and game plans,
So formidable and well executed...

I will continue moving forward,
Carried by momentum,
To the beat of my heart,
And it's impeccable rhythm...

WHAT'S HER FACE?

Get out of my life,
Get away from me,
Get out of my head,
Get moving seriously…

I want to be free,
I want to be clean,
I want to be alive,
I want to be me…

You don't think you are,
But you're a disease,
Just open your eyes,
It's time you believe.

You try to control,
You try to manipulate,
You try to convince,
You totally devastate…

You are a hurricane,
The worst one in history,
You are like standing next to the sun,
You left my soul blistering…

You need to leave me alone,
You need a reality check,
You need to get the hell away,
You need to learn some respect…

I will never return,
I need more than just space,
Can't you tell I'm serious,
By this look on my face...

You love your alcohol,
You love going to clubs,
You love yourself,
You love your drugs...

You are a skunk,
You are a mole,
You are a rat,
You need to get back in your hole...

You tried to stab me,
Five different times,
You got me in the leg,
You got me that one time...

You are dark,
You are from hell,
You are evil,
You are Satan herself...

You can't have my soul,
You can't have this man,
You can't have my life,
You clearly don't understand...

You did one amazing thing,
I will give you that,
You carried my daughter for me,
But that's it, MANIAC!!!

RACE-ISM

Your ignorant mind,
Is confined,
To an existence,
Without equivalence...

What is it that separates,
You and I,
Is it the shade of my skin?
Or is it my different colored eyes?

Or is it because my ancestors,
Mistreated your ancestors?
We can't change the past,
So we should let it go before it festers...

Now I've heard claims that,
One race is superior over the next,
But that sounds like lies,
And a big lack of respect...

Together we stand tall,
All for one and one for all,
We should become "WE",
Because divided we will fall...

Now I love my individuality,
Yet I appreciate diversity,
And if you haven't hurt me,
Then I carry zero animosity...

Don't hate me because,
I'm not the same color of your race,
We need to stop judging one another,
Or war will be our fate...

Is your ignorant mind,
Confined,
To an existence,
Without equivalence?

I have no predetermined opinion,
About you based off your race,
So don't talk down to me,
Or get up in my face...

Racism has existed for centuries,
That's the truth,
But is it really something we,
Should be passing down to our youth?

We should embrace each other,
And stop this violence,
Cops arrest us all the same by saying,
"You have the right to remain silent"...

Just because we have,
Different traditions,
Doesn't justify,
Putting up partitions...

And segregating races,
From our favorite places,
Just because we only want,
To see familiar looking faces?

RAC-ISM

Listen, I know we've had our differences,
On this land,
But at least we have one thing in common now,
We are all Americans!

9/11 united everyone here,
On OUR native soil,
OUR RACE is American now,
The terrorist plot has been foiled…

Because their ignorant minds,
Are confined,
To an existence,
Without equivalence...

FORGIVENESS

We never set out to hold,
A grudge towards another purposely,
However if someone hurts us deliberately or not,
The pain turns into animosity uncontrollably…

I approached this relationship,
Hopeful and unreserved,
With thoughts of the boundless possibilities,
I could experience with her...

Yet I selfishly messed up,
We started fighting frequently,
My actions,
Created problems consequently…

I allowed lies to be told through my lips,
To mask my inability to remain faithful,
I feel guilt but I am driven to cheat,
By an unrecognizable passion that's forceful...

Is it evil? I'm not sure,
However it doesn't matter because I'm compelled to do wrong,
Eventually what we do in the dark comes to the light,
Which in this case didn't take that long…

Even though I felt I was untouchable,
Or that the rules did not apply to me,
Quickly my infidelity was revealed,
For all around me to see...

FORGIVENESS

What is so discouraging,
Is for those who prefer to be on the good side and live right,
They will undoubtedly come across,
Someone that will deceive them in this life...

If by chance,
You have a heart,
Then you will feel guilt,
From lying or getting caught...

If you hurt someone that you have deep feelings for,
It's excruciating,
Witnessing the pain you have caused them,
Is devastating...

The break up inevitably happens and the paths,
That once ran congruent separate as we experience shame,
Now we each continue down our own individual courses,
Yet the haunting memories remain...

I must forgive,
Myself,
However I realize the burden I carry is for the pain I've caused,
Someone else…

I bear this tremendous,
Weight,
And I weep for a scorn woman who most definitely,
Aches...

I am not happy without her,
And part of me wants it to be salvaged,
The other part realizes that no matter what,
It's permanently damaged…

We argue, she screams,
She hits me, she hates me, she flips,
Equipped with only a direct blessing from God,
Will I be fortunate enough to save this friendship?

The passion that once flowed,
Like a raging river has turned into a dried up creek,
I obviously destroyed something,
Wonderful and unique...

Slowly but surely the years grind away,
The outer layer of my emotional steel shroud,
My hopeful relationship lies deep within,
Each conversation and text message that she allows...

She eventually openly forgives me,
And enables me to realize that learning forgiveness was my fate,
This creates a new existence between two souls,
That most definitely are mates...

I must learn from my mistakes,
Retrospect ends,
I now can turn to my future,
Smiling, we develop into best friends…

I now have learned,
Forgiveness is our greatest gift,
Because without it we,
Internally suffer from distress,

I started out seemingly,
Heartless,
However I was blessed with a gift,
The gift of forgiveness...

FORGIVENESS

MY DAUGHTER

Unique curly hair,
Beautiful brown eyes,
Cutest little laugh,
Sweet as apple pie...

You seem to be growing up,
Way to fast,
Soon you will be,
Learning in class...

You are only three now,
Kebi Marie,
There are already so many,
Great memories...

You are an angel,
Brought into this world,
In the form of the most,
Amazing little girl...

I watch as you learn,
Every single day,
I watch as you observe,
I listen to what you say...

I wonder what your favorite,
Interests will be,
Your best subjects in school,
I can't wait to see...

Great sense of humor,
Fun and so bright,
I love telling The 3 Bears,
Every single night...

Intelligent and kind,
You love playing music,
You can be anything you want to be,
I know you can do it...

I will always work hard,
So I can provide,
A strong future for you,
You bring purpose to life...

BEST OF BOTH WORLDS

Walking and talking,
Can be plain mechanical,
So I think and evolve,
To become intellectually spiritual...

It's this voice inside of me,
That's asking deep questions,
Then my body takes me to,
All of its desired destinations...

We work together,
My body and soul,
I am on a great mission,
To increase depth and grow...

I thrive to think differently,
Than originally taught,
Step out of my way,
I go straight through roadblocks...

I will never move backwards,
Just continue to flow,
Live Life is my motto,
Grateful as I reach every goal...

I refuse to make noise,
That should not be heard,
So I carefully express my purpose,
Spoken Through Words...

POEM SUMMARIES

SUMMARY of "HUMILITY"

A young male cannot graduate to manhood until he has experienced a negative consequence of his actions and fully accepted the outcome. A man is humble, understanding that we are not invincible. Humans have a finite life span. Take a moment and ask, "Am I humble?" The answer to this one question will often mark a distinct position on the timeline of life. If the answer is "No," then it most likely is because of youth or inexperience. One must not be humiliated to be humbled; it is just how it happened to me.

The lessons of my past give me strength. Each experience has played a role in defining my identity. Strength is found because I know that who I am is derived from my past. The lessons learned over the course of my life have defined me.

Real men walk with inner-strength. Taking responsibility offers the freedom to hold our head up high because the shame of our past is released. With the right perspective about growth and moving forward, we are more readily equipped to be held accountable for our mistakes.

Personal pride is not living without fault. It simply means being flawed is not an excuse to lie down or give up the fight. We must focus on developing our good qualities while working out the kinks. The easiest way to hold true to this path is by not blaming others for our errors.

The image of the handprint and finger print was chosen because these are unique to each individual. The moment after humiliation, the hand yells, "Stop! Who am I?" An identity crisis immediately ensues causing us to once again rebuild ourselves. The will to continue living as a flawed man shows courage.

SUMMARY of "CRUSH"

We have all had a crush. Crushes make me feel anxious like a young boy. The innocence of the adolescence vibe immerses me in freedom and youth. A new crush reminds me of the radiance of the summer sun warming my skin. I feel safe.

When I was young, the familiarity of the poem "Roses are red" always rolled off my tongue. The rhythm of the poem is the foundation for 'Crush.' A very safe feeling for me is infatuation. By harnessing the familiar rhythm of the traditional poem combined with the safety of feeling infatuation, my aim was to express something very personal to me.

I chose this particular picture because each color of a rose has significance. Red roses are typical to love while pink roses symbolize romance or happiness. Yellow roses stand for friendship and joy while orange roses communicate desire and enthusiasm. The darkest rose, also referred to as a "black rose," says farewell. By saying farewell, we also say hello to new beginnings. Appropriate for a crush don't you think? A crush possesses so much hope and excitement, endless possibilities and outcomes. Every event ends as well. The range of symbolism encapsulated in a rose is very fitting with the experience of a crush.

SUMMARY of "MY PARENTS"

My parents are good people. Through the years, they have provided many wonderful opportunities to me and my sister. Their guidance and connections have opened many doors for me as well. Our family has never had a shortage of love. The piece explores how parents can lose focus on family when their own troubling issues between each other take precedence.

My parents developed an awful excuse for a marriage. It turned violent. The endless arguments and intense fighting made them oblivious to the developing minds of their children. As most children of troubled marriages know, not much goes unnoticed.

The animosity they had for each other after their divorce is still a vivid memory. The bitter comments toward each other found a path for delivery through my sister and me. The greatest loss of their divorce was turning the sacred relationship between a child and a parent into a tool for warfare. The end result was both offensive and confusing.

We never accepted their tactics against one another. Watching them constantly disrespect each other created a deeper divide between them as parents and us as their children. We sought refuge in other places without guidance. My parents' behavior created an environment that fueled our bad behavior.

Fast forward to my life now as a parent and I have learned from their mistakes. The unpleasant cycle has stopped with my child.

An image of a family tree was chosen for this poem. As the family tree continues to grow, it expands and becomes stronger. Pruning the negative out is painful and can damage the infrastructure. But, in order to move forward and achieve success, we must acknowledge the parts of our own family experiences that we often do not want to look at. Our strength comes from accurately reflecting our history and reconciling it with our behaviors of today.

SUMMARY of "REASONS"

Religion is faith in God. I have a strong belief in Jesus Christ. Exploring various perspectives on religion through formal classes has highlighted a common belief in a higher power.

Religions other than Christianity are not wrong, though Christian views are the strongest in my life. God created his only Son to walk amongst us and die for our human sins. The methodology used when engaging in religious teachings can be overwhelming and at times a bit too aggressive. However, the strength of faith is the most powerful human expression.

Religious wars have been constant for thousands of years, proof that the differences in belief can agitate people enough to make them fight. No one likes to be controlled by another's ideology, just ask a teenager with parents. Religion is a personal choice. The experience of my religious beliefs has produced a feeling of completion within my heart.

This poem expresses my love and passion for my beliefs and His saving power. Miracles have occurred in my life that I attribute to direct blessings from God. My hope is that this message will reach out to any person who might be lost. The respect and admiration to my Creator and his Son hopefully show through.

Truth in Christianity is expressed through faith. By following Christianity, the way that I express truth is faith in God. This truth requires no physical proof. I chose this picture because it represents Jesus reaching down from heaven to the people that are choosing to follow him.

SUMMARY of "MISREPRESENTATION"

I found myself in a relationship with a very sweet, beautiful young lady. She convinced me that she was spectacular and a flawless person. At the time, she was a gift. This woman was the first woman I felt serious about since my daughter's mother ("What's Her Face.")

There were many emotions running around in my heart at the time. Bad karma left from my marriage ("Forgiveness") still lingered in my life. She ended up being a wolf in sheep's clothing possessing every last attribute that I would ever dream of. Unfortunately she did not come equipped with a crucial element, faithfulness. After being lied to, I lost trust.

The relationship lasted because of her promises. The original wound never healed properly causing a high level of frustration between us. When we broke up, it devastated me because our relationship died before it should have. I forgive her, however she is too risky to give my full heart to.

The cadence of this poem is quick. Thinking of her makes me want to release my feelings aggressively. The idea of her interrupting me tarnishes the complete picture of pain that I feel. She broke my heart.

This picture represents her in our relationship because she wore a mask. The beauty and mysteriousness of her camouflage distorted my ability to see clearly. Fortunately this relationship has taught me that trust is earned through an individual's actions.

SUMMARY of "THIS IS JUST SEX"

This poem was inspired from events that happened as a bachelor. While single, much of my time and energy is focused on woman and dating. It gets a bit out of control, but the intensity finds a home with me. While in this frame of mind, I hunt for physical compatibility. My appetite for the opposite sex is what I'm attempting to satisfy. However, I am always surprised by the power of chemistry and how it can develop deeper feelings. I love the process of finding meaningful relationships.

This poem is intended to have a powerful flow, showing poise and control. Yet in the end the experience is more than I bargained for and becomes consuming; the feeling of being powerless and blindsided by something so unpredictable. The experiences of pursuing love through lust have shaped a key part of how I search for women to become close to.

The image shows two figures enthralled in what could be described as physical, yet passionate sex. The artist clearly captures an intimate moment. The art has motion and portrays magnetism deeper than the flesh. The mind can't stop with just a kiss on this woman's neck.

SUMMARY of "EVIL LURKS"

Negative forces surround us at all times. Our progress and wellbeing are constantly threatened. The battle between good and evil will always exist. Have you ever noticed the moment positive opportunities are presented in our lives, we simultaneously encounter some kind of negative situation? These attempts are aimed directly at our weaknesses. However, my faith is strong and deep rooted.

Like most people, I have failed countless times. Through the years I have become more aware of the devil's path to my sinful desires. I will not lose these battles any longer.

I chose this picture simply because I see the eyes of an evil creature. We can't stop his tactics. However, possessing this knowledge hopefully negates a sneak attack...

SUMMARY of "PROGRESSION"

This poem was inspired by a moment of revelation triggered by the music of a wind chime. I reminisced on the New Year's resolutions I had organized nine months before. I realized that each one of them had been met and/or had serious progress. The premise here is to set goals and follow through with them one by one. Furthermore, I wanted it to be understood that taking time to set the goals in the first place, followed by acknowledging them when they are completed, can be a momentous occasion in itself. I could feel me, from nine months prior, standing next to myself and smiling.

I chose the picture because at that particular high point in my life, the world did feel like it was right in my hands. We should all take the initiative to create a list of yearly goals then strategize appropriately to reach them. Additionally, we should all aim to attain proud parents, children and followers. The world is ours to respect, utilize, and most of all flourish in.

SUMMARY of "WHAT'S HER FACE"

This poem was created with a slow yet strong beat in mind. My verbal punches and kicks at a person that completely disheveled my self-esteem.

I realized that there was no longer hope in salvaging any level of relationship with her. I pushed her out of my life as quickly as possible. I soon realized that my best path towards healing came in the form of writing and performing this piece.

Most can relate to these words based on their own personal experiences. It doesn't necessarily have to be an exact duplication of anyone else's scenario. It's a fact that we all have an ex that simply needs to stay out of our lives. These specific individuals bring out the worst in us.

Oddly enough, the most painful series of episodes in my lifetime also birthed my wonderful daughter. In darkness, I was blessed with light. In hell, God gifted me with an angel.

The picture captures a man's rage and frustration similar to mine. This man appears to have exploded like a pot of boiling water that moments before, had a lid on it. It is truly amazing how simply writing down words in an organized fashion can help release bottled up emotions that could not be relieved in any other form. Therapy...

SUMMARY of "RACE-ISM"

First of all, the title is purposely hyphenated because I want the word "RACISM" to be part of our past. We can just install the "ISM" on any other number of words. Almost all of the major conflict on this planet today and in our history has sprung from race or religious issues.

I'm serious when I say this has to stop. I believe that racism is a completely outdated and ignorant path of thought. I challenge each and every person to refrain from judging people based on race or religion. Ask yourself right now, "Do I want to be judged negatively based on my race and religion?" Clearly the answer is "No."

We are all different. That's what is so wonderful about us humans. I don't want to look like everyone. I love our wide variety of cultures. Languages and accents should be embraced. The different clothing and music add flair to what would otherwise be a bland existence. Holidays and religious rituals enhance our beautiful diversity.

I'm just totally perplexed with all the violence that has occurred because of our different race interactions. I can understand an argument over a parking spot or a confrontation over a comment involving my woman or child. However, I can guarantee that I wouldn't want someone in my face yelling at me because I'm Caucasian or Christian. My heritage is Irish and Cherokee Indian. I guess if I feel the need to be racist, I simply could get mad at myself, thus creating a terrible way to have an endless inner conflict.

The Europeans traveled by boat to the Americas and forced the natives off their own soil and/or slaughtered them. I feel that the manner in which the natives were almost completely annihilated is absolutely disgusting. However, the least productive way to handle such a situation is by being angry at the world. Therefore, I live for today and tomorrow. I suggest we all work together to avoid another genocide.

The picture represents the human race. It shows people from all walks of life performing numerous tasks. Each silhouette could be anyone. Each silhouette is everyone.

SUMMARY of "FORGIVENESS"

I had the pleasure of being married to one of the finest human beings on the planet. Unfortunately, I was not as ready to be married as I first thought.

This poem speaks of the journey into my raw emotions through that relationship. Specifically, this poem relates to the ending of the marriage and the transformation into friendship. I was very fortunate to be forgiven by her. I am blessed to have her as my best friend now. I understand so much more about life and relationships after all my experiences thus far. It's clear to me that forgiveness is the most selfless gift that God has blessed us with. Only a truly mature person can forgive and reconcile.

Thank you Judy!

The picture speaks sorrow with the initial look. Upon deeper thought, one sees that it displays the first moment of reconciliation. It is very important to forgive people although it is not for the meek. Do not forget that we can't change the past. In turn, accept the past and move forward. We can live without the burden of frustration, anger or sadness though this method.

The picture shows two people that clearly prefer to stay in each other lives so that new memories can be made. Life is simply way too short to carry grudges.

SUMMARY of "MY DAUGHTER"

Many things will change about my daughter over the coming years and our connection will grow. The bond between father and daughter is a special one. I feel blessed to be her father as she is a true joy.

The intent of this poem was to capture the moment in time when my daughter was three. My objective was to describe her personality and how I feel about her. Although expressing my adoration for her is important to do on paper, it is much more crucial as a parent to express my love through actions of discipline and support. Attention to her life will always be a priority. I will not however, stop there. Education through books and respected mentors play an important role in the raising of my child. Parenthood is not a part-time gig. It is a full-time job with a lifetime commitment. Even with the overwhelming commitment, it is also an amazing gift.

The picture of father and daughter walking together hand-in-hand is beautiful. When my daughter becomes an age where holding hands with Dad isn't fun or cool anymore, one thing will still be true. She will still be my baby girl.

SUMMARY OF "BEST OF BOTH WORLDS"

The inspiration behind this poem, which also titles the book, is the relationship between my body and soul. We are one, yet we are separate entities. We co-exist.

Ancient Egyptians believed we had this type of design although their belief was a bit more complex. They seemed to be focused more on the afterlife. Because they would be traveling back and forth between this world and the next, they had to keep their soul connected to the deceased body to live eternally. That is why mummification was such a huge part of their culture. Their existence is referred to as the "Name" (body) and the "Ba" and the "Ka" (soul/spirit). The body and soul actually meet at the birth of the body.

The majority of the world's religions teach about an afterlife; a place where our soul travels after death. I do not reference the next place that my soul will go in this poem although I felt it appropriate to discuss a few interesting beliefs in this summary. My specific purpose of this poem is to show the compatibility of the two. The body is merely a vessel for the much more important soul inside of it. Strength lies within this poem and I feel its power because there is a sense of immortality.

I believe that each of us serve a purpose. I know one of my purposes is to share my experiences with my voice and writing. I view this particular life as one of many journeys to come. So I strongly suggest to you, LIVE LIFE.

The picture is of a physically strong man and his soul wrestling. His soul seems to want to fly away, yet he holds onto it because he can't exist on this planet without it.

OUTRO

WHEW! What a ride! If you are reading this, it signals you have made it through these pages and have momentarily walked in my shoes. I'm not sure that's a good thing, nor a bad thing, nevertheless it just happened.

Starting from this moment on, I suggest leaving each situation in your life as a stronger, smarter, and more prepared person. Never be afraid to grow as a person and certainly leave doubt behind as you walk out the door and into the world. We are all human beings and we have all made mistakes. Despite all that, we must continue to dream big.

For each of us, having purpose in life is defined differently. However, we are forever connected by a common bond and that bond is our range of emotions. If you feel the need to change something about yourself, then do it. Regardless, embrace your personality for what it is. Most importantly, be grateful to God for the gifts you have received from His gracious hand. I know I forever am...

Dustin "INTRIGUE" Doan

My name is Dustin Doan. I was born is Dallas, Texas on February 23, 1977. I have always chosen to live my life by learning it hands on as I go. Although my elders would tell me their stories and try to warn me of common mistakes, I still made my own decisions. I honestly never really listened to authority and it certainly caused me to experience somewhat of a bumpy ride. A rebel without a cause is an appropriate statement. I made it through the storm and now I spend my time on a variety of different activities. I have spent 13 years in the construction and real estate investment businesses. I write and perform poetry. I act in plays and films, and most of all I am a father to an amazing daughter.